Is my curiosity mechanical? Yes,

my own body is a defeated animal.

Ahsahta Press
Boise, Idaho
2017

The New Series
#80

华 诗 画
Hua Shi Hua

[DRAWINGS AND POEMS FROM CHINA]

Jen Hyde

Ahsahta Press, Boise State University, Boise, Idaho 83725-1525
Cover and book design by Janet Holmes
Cover artwork by Patrick Delorey
ahsahtapress.org
Copyright © 2017 by Jen Hyde

LIBRARY OF CONGRESS CATALOGING-IN-PUBLICATION DATA

Names: Hyde, Jen, 1985- author.
Title: Hua shi hua : drawings & poems from China / Jen Hyde.
Description: Boise, Idaho : Ahsahta Press, 2017. |
Series: The new series ; #80 | Includes bibliographical references.
Identifiers: LCCN 2017000358| ISBN 9781934103715 (pbk. : alk. paper) | ISBN
1934103713 (pbk. : alk. paper)
Classification: LCC PS3608.Y366 A6 2017 | DDC 811/.6—DC23
LC record available at https://lccn.loc.gov/2017000358

华话
化花

CONVERSATION

华话   China changes

化花   the flowers say

华话   speaking Chinese

化花   transforms the flowers

CONTENTS

话

Speaking

华

China

化

Transform

花

Flowers

话

CORRESPONDENCE FROM
THE YELLOW CRANE TOWER

TO CUI HAO:

Their people mounted the yellow crane
but who is freer at the top? The yellow crane
has been moving for a while, or is already
gone by the time my word arrives
that white clouds have emptied the air

forever. Finally, the clear day appears
over a clear crater lake.
    Hello Cui Hao,
from this world where the tree of life
is a fragrant Bizarro of your life.

Tell me where the sun sets over your mountains.
From the crane I am saying goodnight, day
falling over the water
the worry are drops, like Visine
lightening the dust from your eyes.

TO LI BAI:

Look west the yellow crane
or a bird I have renamed

you Li Bai you blossom
air out of air

I am still chasing
a fire with a purpose

whose lonely cry is yellow
over the mountain then brown

over the mountain the mountain
adrift the delta an opening into the blue

you prescribed horizons and I
am looking out for a change in the line

from flat to tower did you ever
think of fish when you lifted the river

over your face when the wine spoiled
when the moon too big and yellow grew

TO ZHENG BANQIAO
FROM DONGTING LAKE:

Zheng Banqiao,

What rebuilds the sky
from ground zero
but a courtyard?

From here the yellow crane
swings its mouth over the trees.
Between fists of air

I grasp a blossom. Fruit
has been waiting
for my human hand.

The sun always signals the day
is falling over the mountains again.
The fish in the Yangzte are passing

through the ship locks, free.
And heaven is silver, floating
in the water you immortalized.

TO LI BAI:

Be careful when you tell the doctor
the yellow crane tower cries.

I climbed here to blow wind through a lute
but sat on a short stool, hovered,

Huangshan over small plastic toys.
Li Bai, be a guest in my paper house.

Through mulberry curtains I am shaping
the moon by curling my fingers together.

This is a home that wants to be
a wooden house. Tomorrow I will

leave the lute and the yellow crane,
flown off to find you smelling plums.

FOR MENG HAORAN:

I am a guest and you are the moon
the lute played in the apartment
upstairs.

Or you collaged the awful world
to bear it as the life we have,
the pen as a wind instrument.

How do you lift the cold from
the sea when glass blocks fall?
And where have I been meanwhile?

I am lying in a boat, pushing my mind
into your lake   I once floated with
my curved back in water.

Now I can count alone.
I can watch blankets glide down from
a high-rise window

but I cannot say *blanket*
clear across to my neighbor.
Maybe this is prosperity

the mountains brought you
when finally you shout
from the yellow crane.

华

THE FLOWER PEDDLER

He stopped to light fire to
a paper television and a car.

Sent to another heaven
she receives the chrysanthemum

and jasmine tendered
by his hands. They breathe

the air her box
contains. We cultivate

the truest blue the sky
shows in winter. But he

does not open his coat
when the sun comes. *I flew*

into a bed of stargazer lilies, he says,
I believed she had returned home.

THE CONSTRUCTION
OF A MECHANICAL CRANE

In a hangar in Baoshan Steel City
twenty miles northwest of Shanghai

a worker sleeps in a truck bed
beside machines. To come here is

to say I will look at light
through simple trees, count

the dust masks I have been given
to see

iron particles syphoned
into ivy tunnels

and the machines that cast
the machine I know

as crane.
In the hangar its torso, hollow,

tree-sized, spins
into a screw thread

to form itself. In Shanghai,
when the crane lifts a glass pane

across the sky,
this man dreams a room

rises from a hole in the ground.
I step inside it while another crane

cuts through a cloud.
Is my curiosity mechanical? Yes,

my own body is a defeated animal.
The next day I read

a red-crowned crane in captivity
has lost half her beak.

I return to the factory to wake
the man from his dream.

He prints a titanium
replicate, attaches it

to her injury. As I watch him,
my own mouth stings—

Grey sky in particle matter
press starlight back into stars

but color in trinkets, blue
in the tarp we walk beneath

and listen to, breathing
between double-wide lanes.

The public bus brought me here.
A man with a bled eye searches

for stain-free t-shirts. I sift
through his cart alongside him

for a white size while in the galaxy
meteors drift across our backs. Bird

of light, pushing through fire,
meet the earth in his slender hand

breaking change. He returns
home with something for dinner.

ROCKS FOR I.M. PEI

the cultivated garden
is reduced to rocks

when the wind blows
sunlight into morning

the rocks appear one dimensional
the painting you step into

a building, a machine
a composite metal

sculpture preserved
then recorded

YUYUAN LU

Through a gate, below
pink laundry strung

across the alley,
four men play mahjong.

When their tiles click I hear
a crane lift tiles

to the forty-second story
of a building in the distance.

LAO CHEN

Under fluorescent light she stores
grains, peppers, & beans, red,
green, & white. Her husband and son

sort & divide the food. When she sees
my manufactured heart injury she grips
my forearm, pulls her shirt down and

reveals a scar that resembles mine.
It is a thick line dividing my left breast
from my right. Lao Chen tells me,

Who we love keeps us alive. She presses
two fingers to her chest and says,
Jian your Chinese heart beats inside.

AGRICULTURE

Return me
earth to earth.

As rosemary and carrot
round weevils and wireworms writhe

in tender greens and bitter melon
with black chicken bone marrow

collagen. I unfold bird
wings in my mouth and

raze the fields.
I am wild.

My wings slice
into the face

I have been trying to conjure.
She emerges from the rice

to hold my heart
in your palm, in the food

which is food
the earth loves

so much it gives me—
practically—away.

RAPID CITY

My tool for splitting land
arrived and terraced the sea.

Now I have a hundred bent
elbows bending, drinking tea.

What home deteriorates
under rain? Into silver slithers

I watch you coax the river. My own
song within the parameters

of the walls who sing, *we
were just under construction.*

Do you hear the other whispers? Even
hushed, a voice remains unfrozen,

says, *from water ice
fractures the sky.* Hanging

stars jacket our bare camp and ask,
who enhances the sport of falling?

We wait in quiet for their answers
and feel wind brush our trousers.

I think you are saying
the apple is pixilated

solid washed
red and flat.

That you know the shit
river smell. The sly

storm approach. That I
nearly boarded a bus.

Let me tell you
about the Xinjiang jujube.

Coarse and seedless propagated
fruit receives help from a bee.

He pollinates
meteor showers.

I count one star
in the Shanghai sky. But

there is fire, and volley, and a curled tin
fish's spin within the silk trade.

DINGXI LU

Show me the fluffy animals' history
and their escape from the zoo:

> The water logged in high-heeled shoes
> that up from tiled sidewalks pool into
> right angles made in filigree.

Tell me about the lion's courage
and the brown bear's haunches—

> *I am* the hipster pirate mouse.

Out of the crane do we emerge
as creatures?

> In my room, lit silver,
> I eat crayfish eyes

I think the river treasures
the sea, a capsule.

A man casts his line toward Puxi
and the river fish swarm to his bait.

Their mouths, hooked open,
die in sunlight. Yesterday

the cranes spread
over this water

to build more infrastructure.
When a mirror faces another

mirror I think
a new room opens

across the river.
But he does not cross over.

AFTERWARD (后序后)

I

What is this line but breathless length the sun assembles through the trees? The geodesic
light?   Bramblings descend in clusters and bounce   tenderly when they land.
On our ride their breeze brushes my skin. I am light with the air I was just shouldered by
so much unused Styrofoam   mounted to a scooter.

II

We ascend the façade of the Lavazza café to find   a plane of grass on which two men
draw figure eights in the sky with their kites. They play the breeze in cadence with dump
truck percussion and you say it is new-wave opera.   The story is of the phoenix' descent
into a peony   a fuchsia brocade on red silk   a lucky red button   unlatched from an old
woman's collar. She sings metrical, isochronous hinge, auxiliary cleaves   immutable blue
below a green valley. In the new glass city   corn is an insulation. The husked hulls
we see, the shackled glass doors, the suggestion of coffee, prepare this cranes   to fly above
my specular reflection.   Into a diffuse sunrise, into the hollow world.

III

Grecian busts form a wall near the house paint market. I walk past the marriage market.
Below it, the wedding dress market.   Here is grandma's work.   She imagines, sews gems
onto lace princesses and bejeweled trumpets and veils.   To red shoes and silver shoes   I
find no blue shoes. I am in a market with my loneliness.   I am in the insect and bird
market.   Then the market for giant woks.   In the eyeglass market a man soaks my optic
lens   until I see the night market closed.   I believe I see a sequins market.   In the fabric
market I find nylon threaded through cashmere.   In the pearl market watch   the vendor,
now a magician, scrape away   my opalescent façade.

23

I V

In your printed manuscript. In your aerial vesper write the notes a ghost cannot follow.
Tomorrow I am a sequined moon princess selling split onions. When chickens finish laying
eggs I carry them back to the house. On a heap of eggplant, watermelons sprout.
I buy these in a warehouse, in a stall near the stockings and bump-its—

V

But I am a terrible bargainer. Somewhere between the market for new ideas and a market of
superb dreams, is a market of superior goods, a market of barges and cranes. In the
market for people who want to try doing something different everyday you smell of flowers,
taste earth. We have been looking at our own map. I learn a few good things should be
carried like the child who wants a pillow but hasn't yet learned to say pillow so we bring
him to the puffy wall and he chooses what his eyes register as lime green.

V I

He is the future city, the inhabitable voice that never asks *did you remember to take your keys*
with you when you left home? There is a new row of condos coming together by the freeway.
Becoming white noise is falling asleep hearing I am never alone and waking
less afraid. I graphed more and more lines in a circle on a sheet labeled earth
to draw my home I know I am somewhere, waiting.

化

AUTUMN NATURE RHAPSODY

The leaves are red and yellow,
the red and yellow leaves are

the leaves, red on top and
yellow underneath. I secretly

see them but say I see
natural scenery offers

a compliment to the trees.
To let language gesture leaves

the yellow and red to be no more
in love with words than the order

of brilliant clovers and ferns that
blanket greens into the season.

YELLOW RHAPSODY

through my window winter air
the yellow   yellow clouds depart
two cranes   or removes blue

from the night sky I wait
to grow, to dance,
to flank and thigh the riverside

to ground my yellow body
my yellow flight. I wait in yellow air
while the road machines a long lullaby.

You hum me into sleep. In stillness and in steel
two cranes are waiting to be dropped.
Tonight from the tower, the leaves are here—

and here comes yellow earth—

A CATALOGUE OF THINGS I KNOW, A JIAN (一个简)

a crane lifting steel
raises my heart
mourning the sky

a crane is a mountain
where two birds meet
to make Earth appear

from the distance
the clearest sound
their echoes cry

I feel my heart
crane from Shanghai
to find you asleep

I want the man
who machines
small beaks

and dismantles cranes
to make me a human
in his sleep

to machine buildings
to leap into the ocean
to collect the crane

who will carry me
home in my body
in the crane's language

I crane my neck
and sing to this woman
but the crane's song

sounds the night
into my bones
a sliver of moon

from further away
sound is a lack
of motion

when the crane sings
hua hua hua hua
my body shivers

I am a woman
announcing her
own form

the crater is a crater
the crane flies below
the crane operator

the ceramics man
casts his thumbprint
into a light box

measure my
bashful light
until we are old

stars lighting
the moon even
in a bad dream

I will not unfold
when I am Jen
I am a book a 简

& bicycle pedals
& the crane
& the tower tipping the sky

from a mountain
gravel descends
into a wetland

we step in mud and
over a wet rock
to set the crane

into the moon
he says you
are not white-washed

AUTUMN NATURE RHAPSODY, REVISED

I know how the red and yellow leaves
hold up the gray ninety-degree angles
affixed to the sky. With pants

hanging out of windows
in the high rise. Dear leaves,
you must pull winter

into the machined world we
only thought the Internet could dream.
When stars light the evening

cloud drifts are calling, *reach up*
toward heaven and fall gently down.
I color my prayer on this ground.

IN THE YEAR OF THE OX

I opened my mouth
into a door frame,
an exit, a kou—a horse

razing orange over
slow cranes at work
becoming as air raids

that begin morning
exercise. I count
to eight, call myself

a grove of trees,
a hybrid lemon and
tangelo, a fruit

that just isn't right
for lemonade.
I was born a cow.

YAK

I recently
had my
heart opened
and now

dream I
am a sleepy
panda gnawing
on bamboo.

I wonder
if I'm really trying
to return
to China

in these dreams
as an iron-
deficient bear
to retrieve

my discovery of
something new.
I dream I
reinvent China

as a snow-globe
I haven't shaken
nor footslogged
by train or bus lately.

A place where Dai
people are fowl, beasts
and melons sunning
their porch meat.

Their street
snacks burn
my mouth but
I don't have hands

to shake this world
upside down and
make ice pellets
fall. I don't have

a scar trickling
down my chest.
Nor many
holes where

my pleural
effusions drained
quietly this year, no.
But below

my skin there's
a new bovine
heart sack.
I must not be

a panda. Rather
a yak, licking
the inside of
this glass vessel.

Last year my heart
ventured above the sea
and still beats. Twenty
days ago they laid me

on a table with
an oxygen mask
over my mouth.
I breathed in

a girl running
through rapeseed
from the worm's
view. My legs

move flowers
right to left
past so
much sky.

I was headed
nowhere which
I imagine is the
act of moving

toward heaven.
Time is
still while
they embroider

chrysanthemums
on your neck
and bouquets bloom
on you, Yak.

They manipulate
your body in
anomalous
positions and fashion

a patchwork organ.
You'll wake functional.
Your heart will be
new. You can speak

the same poor
foreigner Chinese
you are making
tiny *progresses*.

SELF-PORTRAIT

Looking at my picture
I whisper

        I am an I

        from my mother
        who never
        says I.

        I am an I

She would have discarded

our Chinese embroideries
if she let herself   claim *I*

        ration rice and trade cotton the sea
        gypsies pass from ocean to island.

        I am an I

        in an eyelash in my hand
        while the cranes move in the city.

Then I count the hours
I hated plastic
covering our chairs.

I came into *I*
in damaged fabric sales, the Costco
codes, an app we cannot see, a coupon for free

pictures the Internet shows.
Our country was a beautiful home they cleaned up well.
In High Definition we touched a holy temple

but the view is not a perspective to hold onto.

but in the photo of your small body
folded at the edge of a bed
I look back and say *I will walk into the next day.*

HER SHOULDER IS A SHELTER

Until now we had been looking at pictures
of tree-lined lanes and sun

shimmering between leaves.
She paints sight as moving color

to break open the world.
Over downy cloud clusters

I see her blue
lit corridors

press into other rooms.
I am looking at pictures on a very large

chair. There are no dragons here, only
the white walls my mother wipes daily.

Her shoulder is a shelter on which we arrange
rock formations to resemble skin burdens.

One of three who is one of none
who are the thin newspaper cuts

she collages Sunday coupons and pen
women hand in hand?

She marks
who is who.

I dream I am a bird
but here I am a rabbit

or a bear drawn
with a heart-shaped

nose and anchor mouth. These
torn papers are stacked in a box.

They are envelopes
and birthday notes.

Hello,
I type to her over the Internet.

It is nice to write
you in a cached textbox.

I watched you leave this summit
where you began as a guest.

There are fragrant leaves over there
I dream a woman speaks.

I reply to her, standing
in a cabinet while silkworms

crack open their cocoons
in the time a mountain occupies.

I am peering on a quiet night, alone
with the moths, unable to fly.

花

RED PEONY

When her body escapes her spirit flies
as a red-crowned crane into the night.
Your hand reaches toward her but glass
eclipses you from touching her wings.
Look now at your embroidered robe
and trace a peony bloom into the silk
sky that cloaks your body to recall
the life she opened, the life she was.

In the morning, please return
the light and speak of flowers
blooming flowers, of mist swooping
mist into the valley. Here, your new
home sits under clouds and above a
butterfly that moves across a rapeseed
field. But you are also the field.
When the cold morning wakes you,
cornered by mice and mites, pose
yourself on yellow flowers. They are
your flowers now.

You tell me your stalks are
wooden and winter, bare.
Tell me instead cranes will rest
here. Tell me lettuce and field
arrange heaven. Who says
I cannot send you flowers? That
your genus is chiffon, and silk—
Look, I look my best with your
flowers. Look at your flowers dying
in my hair, now look I am
thanking you for my light.

Now I know the red and yellow leaves
don't compare to concrete and water,
or to you watching me mouth your word
for cranes. My tongue parses rust from scrap
metal. At dawn I tell you your head
is the moon, that you have been—all along—
the milky light who sings me into another body.

NOTES
AND ACKNOWLEDGMENTS

NOTES AND ACKNOWLEDGMENTS

The characters 华话化花 sound very similar in Mandarin; one says "hua."

诗画, *shihua*, or landscape and poetry is a form of classic Chinese drawing and painting.

The sections of "Correspondence from The Yellow Crane Tower" are generative translations of the following poems: "Yellow Crane Tower" by Cui Hao, "On Yellow Crane Tower Hearing a Fute" by Li Bai, "Dongting Lake Autumn Moon" by Zheng Banqiao, "On the Yellow Crane Tower Hearing the Sound of a Flute" by Li Bai, "Seeing Meng Haoren Off at Yellow Crane Tower" by Li Bai (trans. Dongbo, *Mountain Songs*, MIT Database).

"Red Peony" is written in response to the line 花心心籥 from Wang Wei's poem, "Red Peony."

The lines *flowers blooming flowers, mist / swooping mist* in "Plum Blossom" is an image borrowed from the poem "The Bloom is not a Bloom" by Bai Juyi, trans. Witter Bynner, *300 Tang Poems,* Knopf, 1920.

"The River of Yellow Flowers" borrows the title from a line in the poem "A Green Stream" by Wang Wei, trans. Witter Bynner, *300 Tang Poems.*

The poetic motifs employed in these poems respond to Ezra Pound's organizing principles in his collection *Cathay* and Amy Lowell and Alice Ascough's translation collaboration, *Fir-Flowers.*

·

Thanks to the editors of the following journals, where some of these poems first appeared, sometimes in slightly different form: *Drunken Boat* ("Correspondence from The Yellow Crane Tower (to Cui Hao, Zheng Banqiao, Li Bai, and for Meng Haoren)"); *elsewhere* ("Afterward, Hou Xu Hou"); *Likewise Folio* ("Rocks for I.M. Pei," "Yuyuan Lu," "Yu Garden," "Dingxi Lu," and "Celebration Square"); *The Margins* ("The Flower Peddler" and "Her Shoulder is a Shelter"); *The Portable Boog Reader* ("The Construction of a Mechanical Bird," "In the Year of the Ox," and "Red Peony"); *The Sink Review* ("Agriculture" and "Autumn Nature Rhapsody, Revised"); and in "They Will Sew the Blue Sail" in *The Volta* ("Anfu Lu").

"Yak" was first performed in Emotive Fruition in July 2013.

"Correspondence from The Yellow Crane Tower, to Cui Hao" was republished in *The Literary Review* online.

"Afterward, Hou Xu Hou" was a finalist for the prose prize from *elsewhere*.

•

Thank you to Amy Becker, Diane Geng, Marianne Petit, David Perry and my faculty advisor, Eunjoo Kim at NYU Shanghai for your enthusiasm, and for giving me the time and space to produce these poems. To my careful readers and friends, most especially Sarah Sala, Jenny Xie, Emily Brandt, Vivian Xu, Ching-In Chen, Charif Shanahan, Jacob Severn, Brian Trimboli, Gillian Barth, Scott Leinweber and Darcy Allen, and Liv and Jeff Zilberstein thank you for helping me see these poems forward. To my first writing teachers, Christian Hawkey, Jen Bervin, and Daniel Nester, and later writing teachers, Matthew Zapruder, Matther Rohrer, Kimiko Hahn, and Deborah Landau, thank you for teaching me how to build and trust in my own practice.

To the editors of *Drunken Boat*, Anna Rosenwong and Maria Jose Gimenez; Kylan Rice, editor of *The Likewise Folio*; Joshua Marie Wilkinson, editor of *The Volta*; Steven Karl, editor of *The Sink Review*; Thomas Dooley, director of Emotive Fruition; Spencer Hyde, Sam Thayn and Lindsay Webb at *elsewhere* magazine; Paige Taggart and David Kirschenbaum editors of the *Boog City Reader*; and Emily Jungmin Yoon and Jyothi Natarajan, editors of *The Margins*, thank you for giving these poems their first homes.

Thank you to Jyothi Natarajan, Noel Pangilinan, and Ken Chen for supporting me as an emerging writer at The Asian American Writer's Workshop, and thank you, endlessly, Janet Holmes for your time and thoughtfulness and editorial expertise. I am so grateful.

Lastly, thank you to my parents, Bobby and Katherine, for giving me a voice, and to my husband, Patrick, for championing it.

AUTHOR'S NOTE

At the end of 2013 I moved to Shanghai. I wanted to teach myself how to read a language of my heritage and to understand my Chinese identity. In Mandarin I am called a *huaren,* an ethnically Chinese person who was not born in China; in English I am a person of the Chinese diaspora by way of my mother, who moved to the United States from Indonesia. As a biracial American poet and book artist, I have felt illiterate in the language of my own culture—a language that, nevertheless, belongs to me.

In Shanghai, I audited a book arts class taught by Marianne Petit at NYU Shanghai, and I assisted with the launch of university's first student-run news publication. While I experimented with book forms and storytelling, I was learning about free speech in China, a concept more complex than is (or can be) depicted by English-language media. Those complexities shaped the way I began writing about the Shanghai landscape; I became invested in depicting the liminal life moments and interactions and stillnesses between me and the people I encountered in the city, and how such encounters enabled me to think about my own family and cultural history. I began to think about freedom of speech as not just the right to discuss, critique, and advocate for a variety of human voices in a political conversation, but also as one's personal right to her own experience.

Around this time, I began reading about the small press publishing practices in the Ming Dynasty. At that time, the cities around Shanghai were known for producing prolific poetry, and for manufacturing materials (paper, ink, and brushes) to make books. I read the Chinese printing scholar, Chow Kai-Wing, who explained why woodblock printing became a popular and affordable publishing method for small presses in China: despite Gutenberg's development of moveable type in Europe, "woodblock printing remained the most attractive technology to most Chinese printers without substantial resources." Because "a carver did not need to be literate, illiterate workers, including women and children could and did become carvers. A book could be produced by one person—from copying the text to the block, printing copies, and finely stitching up the pages."[1] In Chow's description I felt I'd found myself, a maker of books and an illiterate person who was both inside a cultural landscape I had been born into and outsid

---

[1] Chow, Kai-Wing, "Reinventing Gutenberg: Woodblock and Moveable-Type Printing in Europe and China." *Agents of Change: Print Culture Studies after Elizabeth L. Eisenstein*, edited by Sabrina Alcorn Baron, Eric N. Lindquist, and Eleanor F. Shevlin. University of Massachusetts Press. 2007. pp. 187–190.

of the immediate cultural and historical fluency of that language. I transformed Chow's description into a recorded performance of illiterate book publishing in which I played the role of publisher, printer, and illiterate writer. I printed five copies of this manuscript using woodblock plates, a laser cutter, traditional relief printing techniques, and bamboo paper which I sourced from a paper village in Suzhou. The paper village remains an independent publisher today, though due to copyright and publishing laws in China, it prints only classic texts. They are beautiful.

The poems in this printing of *Hua Shi Hua* are an artifact of my performance. Through a process I call generative translation, I interpreted classic Chinese poetry written at the site of the Yellow Crane Tower in Wuhan City, and I used the image of the crane, whose presence is now that of a machine in the Shanghai skyline, to explore the city's landscape and to find my own relationship to my mother and our heritage as I moved through it. This method of exploration enabled me to render a range of my own selves in the landscape of my poems. As an adult with a congenital heart defect, I have undergone two open-heart surgeries in my lifetime, and I will continue to undergo these procedures as new advancements in the research for my condition are made. I recently received a bioprosthetic heart valve made with the pericaridum tissue of a cow. I was also born in the year of the Ox, an identity that gives me hope in the face of always questioning my health and my right to call myself an Asian American woman. When the speaker of my poems claims she is part animal, she may be reaching for the most literal version of her physical self. This is, at once, armor and armament because the right to a cultural self can be more easily dismissed by others both in the reality of these poems and in real life.

The title of this book draws on four characters that, to the foreign ear, make a similar sound (*hua*), yet each of these characters is distinct in writing and distinguished by its tone when spoken aloud. I used them as an organizing principle for this book, and I combined them to write a bilingual poem. When I finished the performance, I realized that perhaps I am not so much an illiterate writer, but one who is unable to fully understand both my first language and the languages of my heritage, and that this is an identity that requires lifelong mining. In Shanghai, I'd just found the beginning of my work as a poet.

ABOUT THE AUTHOR

JEN HYDE is a poet and occasional book artist. She is a collaborative publisher for ND/SA, the assistant poetry editor of the *Bellevue Literary Review*, and a Heart Valve Ambassador for the American Heart Association. Her work has been supported by fellowships from NYU Shanghai and The Asian American Writer's Workshop where she was a 2016 Margins Fellow. She lives in Brooklyn, New York.

AHSAHTA PRESS

NEW SERIES

AHSAHTA PRESS

SAWTOOTH POETRY PRIZE SERIES

2002: Aaron McCollough, *Welkin* (Brenda Hillman, judge)
2003: Graham Foust, *Leave the Room to Itself* (Joe Wenderoth, judge)
2004: Noah Eli Gordon, *The Area of Sound Called the Subtone* (Claudia Rankine, judge)
2005: Karla Kelsey, *Knowledge, Forms, The Aviary* (Carolyn Forché, judge)
2006: Paige Ackerson-Kiely, *In No One's Land* (D. A. Powell, judge)
2007: Rusty Morrison, *the true keeps calm biding its story* (Peter Gizzi, judge)
2008: Barbara Maloutas, *the whole Marie* (C. D. Wright, judge)
2009: Julie Carr, *100 Notes on Violence* (Rae Armantrout, judge)
2010: James Meetze, *Dayglo* (Terrance Hayes, judge)
2011: Karen Rigby, *Chinoiserie* (Paul Hoover, judge)
2012: T. Zachary Cotler, *Sonnets to the Humans* (Heather McHugh, judge)
2013: David Bartone, *Practice on Mountains* (Dan Beachy-Quick, judge)
2014: Aaron Apps, *Dear Herculine* (Mei-mei Berssenbrugge, judge)
2015: Vincent Toro, *Stereo. Island. Mosaic.* (Ed Roberson, judge)
2016: Jennifer Nelson, *Civilization Makes Me Lonely* (Anne Boyer, judge)

This book is set in Apollo MT type
with Adobe Song and Adobe Ming characters
by Ahsahta Press at Boise State University.
Cover and book design by Janet Holmes.
Cover artwork by Patrick Delorey.

AHSAHTA PRESS
2017

JANET HOLMES, DIRECTOR

PATRICIA BOWEN, *intern*
SAM CAMPBELL
KATHRYN JENSEN
COLIN JOHNSON
DAN LAU
MATT NAPLES